Contents

Eagles

Eagles are among the largest and most powerful of all birds. They are **birds of prey** – large birds that hunt other animals for food. To help them hunt, eagles have a powerful hooked beak, excellent eyesight and feet that end in curved **talons**. Male and female eagles look similar, although the females are usually larger than the males. Eagles are related to hawks, falcons and vultures.

Eagle

The word eagle comes from the Latin word 'aquila', the name given to the golden eagle by the Romans.

fact

This large Verreaux's eagle has a **wingspan** of more than 2m. It swoops down on **prey** animals, which it catches as they run along the ground.

Animal Lives

EAGLES

Sally Morgan

QED Publishing

Written by Sally Morgan
Designed by Q2A Solutions
Editor Tom Jackson
Map by PCGraphics (UK) Ltd

Publisher Steve Evans
Creative Director Louise Morley
Editorial Manager Jean Coppendale

Printed and bound in China

Picture credits

Corbis: Front Cover W Perry Conway, George D Lepp 5, Eric and David Hosking 7, Bettmann 10, Ron Sanford 11, W Perry Conway 13, 23, Joe McDonald 16, Philip Richardson/Gallo Images 18, Uwe Walz 20, Mary Ann McDonald 24, Galen Rowell 29
Ecoscene: Fritz Polking 14, Peter Cairns 24
FLPA: Jurgen & Christine Sohns 1, Winfried Wisniewski 4, 6, 7, Michael Callan 12, Tom and Pam Gardner 21, KLAUS NIGGE/FOTO NATURA 22
Getty Images: Grant Faint/The Image Bank 8–9, Art Wolfe 15, 30, John Warden/Stone 25, Joseph Van Os/The Image Bank 27
Still Pictures: Fritz Polking 17, Gunter Ziesler 19, JEREMY WOODHOUSE/WWI 23, DANIEL DANCER 28, Clyde H Smith 30, Thomas D Mangelsen 30

Title page: Bald eagle

Words in **bold** are explained in the Glossary on page 31.

What's a bird?

Birds have a number of features that make them different from other animals. Their bodies are covered in feathers and they have wings, rather than arms. Female birds lay eggs that hatch into chicks.

Eagles have a hooked beak for ripping flesh.

Eagle types

There are about sixty different species, or types, of eagle. Most eagles are larger and more powerful than other hunting birds, such as hawks. Eagles are divided into four groups: snake eagles, fish and sea eagles, booted eagles and harpy eagles.

The bateleur eagle is a snake eagle. Its name comes from the French word meaning 'acrobat'.

The hawk eagle is a booted eagle. It has short, rounded wings and a rounded tail.

Four groups of eagles

Booted eagles get their name from their thickly feathered legs. Bald eagles belong to the fish and sea eagles group. They usually live near water and catch fish. Snake eagles are small and feed on snakes. Harpy eagles are the largest and most powerful eagles. They live in tropical rainforests.

The greater spotted eagle is a booted eagle. It is about 70cm in length from its head to its tail tip.

Vital statistics

The great harpy eagle has a wingspan of up to 2m and the females may weigh as much as 9kg. One of the smallest eagles is the ornate hawk eagle, which has a wingspan of about 1.2m and weighs less than 2kg.

Where can you find eagles?

Eagles can fly long distances, so they are found in most parts of the world. However, they are not found in some of the more remote islands, such as New Zealand and Antarctica.

Bald eagles can be found in the far north of Alaska and Canada, where they have to survive the long cold winters.

All habitats

Eagles live in almost every type of **habitat**, including deserts, coasts and farmland. Sea eagles and bald eagles are found in the cold Arctic. Harpy eagles live in South American rainforests. The bateleur and martial eagles hunt over the savannah grasslands of southern Africa.

Some eagles have become used to people and have moved into towns and cities. Bald eagles even visit rubbish dumps to look for food.

Eagle

Haast's eagle was the largest bird of prey ever. It weighed more than 20kg and had a wingspan of 2.6m. It once lived in New Zealand, where it preyed on another giant bird called the moa. Both Haast's eagle and the moa are now extinct.

fact

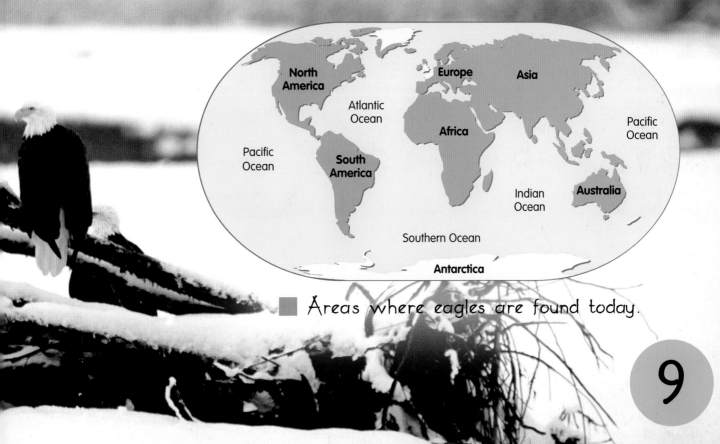

Areas where eagles are found today.

9

Building a nest

Eagles build huge nests in places that are difficult to reach, such as on ledges or high in trees. Eagle nests, also called **eyries**, are made from twigs. The inside is lined with soft grass or leaves.

Eagles return to the same nest every year, adding more twigs each time. Some old nests become so big and heavy that they break the supporting branches and crash down to the ground.

Usually the male eagle collects the twigs and the female arranges them in the nest. It takes weeks, sometimes months, to build a nest.

A male bald eagle dives towards a female during a courtship display.

Courtship

Many eagles mate for life. This means that they live with the same partner until one dies. During their **courtship**, the male eagle brings the female gifts of food. Some males perform a courtship display in which they dive towards the female from great heights or turn somersaults in the air.

Eagle fact

The largest known bald eagle nest was found in Florida. It was 2.7m across, 6m deep, and weighed more than 2 tonnes!

Laying eggs

The female eagle lays between one and three eggs and sits on them to keep them warm. This is called **incubation**. The eggs hatch after about 60 days. The egg that was laid first is the first to hatch. The older chick is larger and grabs more of the food. Often, younger chicks die from starvation or are killed by the eldest chick. At least one of the chicks usually survives.

Young eagle chicks are covered in soft feathers and they cannot fly.

Once the chicks have hatched, the female eagle stays near the nest to guard them. The male brings them food.

Eagle enemies

Adult eagles have few enemies, but the chicks are often killed by snakes, raccoons and other large birds, such as ravens.

Eagle

Young chicks are unable to control their body temperature. They depend on their mother to keep them warm and sheltered from the rain and sun.

fact

Growing up

Young eagles leave the nest when they are about one month old. They cannot fly at this age, so they hop from the nest onto branches or ledges. Then they start to make short flapping jumps. Their jumps get longer and longer, and eventually the young eagles are able to make their first short flight.

Most adult eagles feed their young until they are between three and five months of age. This gives young eagles plenty of time to practise their flying and to learn how to hunt.

The young bald eagle on the right will not grow its adult feathers until it is about three years old.

Young eagles have large wing and tail feathers to help them to fly.

Changing feathers

Young eagles have different coloured feathers from older eagles. Often the young eagles have light and dark brown feathers on their back and paler feathers on their front.

Flying

Eagles are experts at flying. Their wings are long and wide, which helps them to glide. Many eagles can stay in the air for hours and hardly have to flap their wings at all.

A bald eagle flying in the air for an hour will flap its wings for as little as two minutes. This allows the eagle to fly long distances without using a lot of energy.

The eagle's wing feathers are separated at the tips. This helps air to pass over the wing and makes the eagle's flight smoother.

A bald eagle dives at high speeds by folding back its wings. It opens them again to slow down.

Rising high

Eagles rise high into the sky using **thermals**. These are currents of warm air that rise up from the land. Eagles can fly over long distances using thermals. They are pushed up by one thermal and then slowly glide down to catch the next thermal, which takes them back up again.

Eagle

The bald eagle is not really bald. It was named after the white feathers on its head and neck.

fact

Eagle senses

Eagles have amazing eyesight. Their eyes can see at least four times better than a human's eyes. This helps them to spot their prey from high up in the air.

Eagles can see things that people would need **binoculars** to spot. For example, an eagle can spot a rabbit 1500m away. A person could only just see the same rabbit from a distance of 500m.

Hearing

Eagles have a well developed sense of hearing. They listen carefully for the noises made by their prey. However, their sense of smell is poor.

Eagles have a ridge over their eyes that makes them look very fierce, like this monkey-eating eagle.

Unlike human eyes, an eagle's eyes cannot move from side to side. To look around, an eagle has to turn its whole head.

Eagle

If someone says you are eagle-eyed, it means that you spot things that others might not notice.

fact

19

Feeding

Eagles are meat eaters. Most eagles feed on small mammals, such as rabbits and mice, or catch fish. However, snake eagles feed mostly on snakes and lizards. In South America, the harpy eagles feed on a range of animals that live in the rainforest. They use their huge talons to catch monkeys, parrots and lizards in the trees. The slow-moving sloth makes up one third of their diet.

This martial eagle is attacking a warthog. The warthog is defending her babies from the eagle.

This white-bellied sea eagle has carried a fish back to its perch. It holds the fish firmly in its talons, then pulls it to pieces with its beak.

Eagle

Snake eagles have thick scales on their legs and feet to give protection against biting snakes. They attack snakes up to 3m long including cobras, adders and mambas.

fact

Eating their food

Eagles kill their prey with their curved talons. Some eagles then eat their meal on the ground, while others carry it to a perch. Eagles use their hooked beaks to rip their food into chunks.

Hunting

Eagles hunt during the day so they can make the most of their excellent sight. Some eagles sit at the top of a tree or on a cliff ledge watching for prey. They stay perfectly still so that their prey does not notice them. When it spots something, the eagle dives down and grabs it.

Eagle

The bateleur eagle spends most of the day in the air. It takes off as soon as the day warms up and flies almost continuously until the cooler hours of the evening. It can cover up to 300km a day looking for food.

fact

This Steller's sea-eagle has spotted a fish in the water and is about to take off from its perch.

Searching from the air

Other eagles, such as the golden eagle, fly around looking for prey. When they spot an animal, they swoop down and catch it in their talons. Harpy eagles must steer between tree branches to catch their prey. Sea eagles are known as the pirates of the eagle world because they steal prey from other birds.

The eagle uses its powerful hooked talons to catch and carry its prey.

The martial eagle is the largest eagle in Africa. It perches in trees in the early morning and evening. The rest of the time it spends in the air.

23

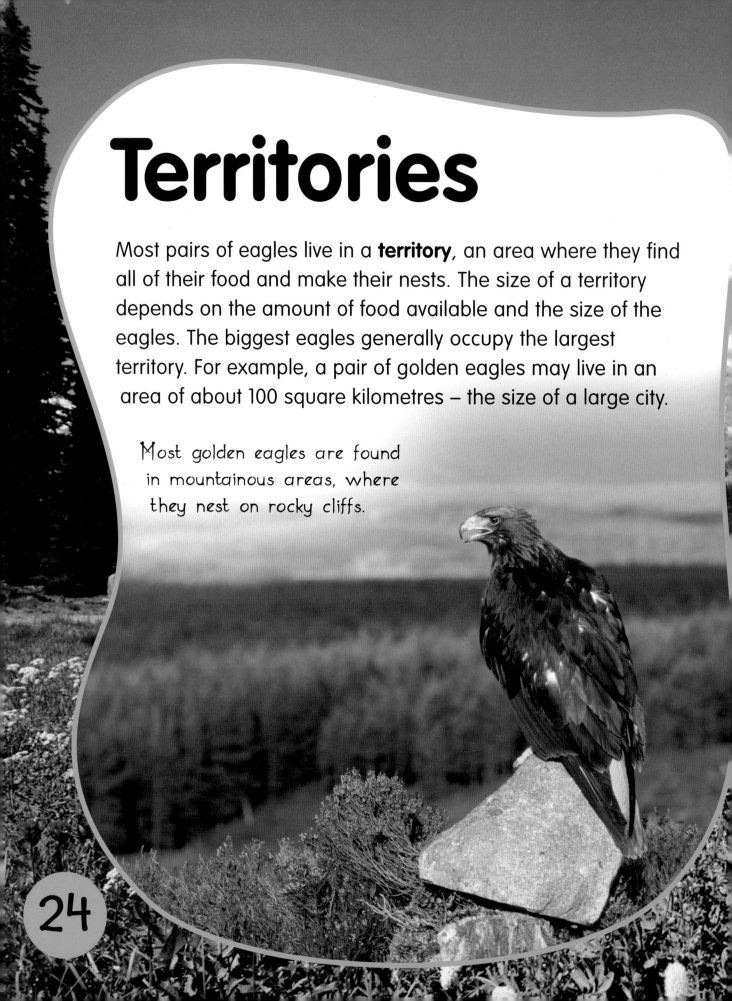

Territories

Most pairs of eagles live in a **territory**, an area where they find all of their food and make their nests. The size of a territory depends on the amount of food available and the size of the eagles. The biggest eagles generally occupy the largest territory. For example, a pair of golden eagles may live in an area of about 100 square kilometres – the size of a large city.

Most golden eagles are found in mountainous areas, where they nest on rocky cliffs.

Fighting other eagles

Eagles defend their territory and chase away intruders. However, younger eagles may not have a territory and so they fly around, passing through the territories of older eagles. If one of a pair of eagles dies during the breeding season, a young eagle will move in and take the place of the dead bird.

Eagle

A group of several eagles soaring in a thermal together is described as a 'kettle of eagles'.

fact

This bald eagle is trying to chase away another adult bald eagle.

25

Eagle communication

Eagles communicate with each other using flight displays and calls. Some male eagles perform diving displays high above their territory to tell others nearby that the area is occupied.

Golden eagles are mostly silent, except during the breeding season. They use nine different calls to communicate.

Bald eagles have a screeching call similar to a seagull's.

Eagle calls

Eagles are normally quiet birds and they cannot sing. But they do use calls to communicate with each other. Their calls are shrill shrieks or high-pitched twitters. Some calls are warnings to other eagles, while other calls are used to attract attention.

Male and female eagles make calls to greet each other at their nest and to call to their chicks.

Eagle

The courtship of the bald eagle includes spectacular displays in which two birds grasp each other's feet high in the air and spin towards the ground, cartwheeling with their wings and legs outstretched.

fact

Eagles under threat

Eagles everywhere are in danger. The main threat comes from the loss of their habitat. For example, forests are being cleared for timber and to make way for new farmland.

Large eagles prey on lambs and game birds, such as pheasants, so they are not always liked by farmers and gamekeepers. In many places, eagles are **poisoned** or shot.

The harpy eagle's habitat is destroyed when tropical rainforests are cut down.

Eagle conservation

One way to save the eagles is to **conserve** their habitat and their nesting sites, especially rainforests. Many countries have laws against killing eagles or collecting their eggs.

These people have travelled a long way to watch bald eagles in Homer, Alaska, in winter.

Eagle

Three species of eagle are very likely to become extinct soon. They are the Madagascar serpent eagle, the Madagascar fish eagle and the Philippine eagle.

fact

Life cycle

Eagles breed once a year. The female lays up to three eggs, which take 60 days to hatch. Young eagles leave their parents when they are about four months old. They begin to breed at between two and nine years of age. Eagles live between 20 to 30 years in the wild and up to 60 years in captivity.

Chick in nest

Older chick leaving nest

Adult eagle

Glossary

binoculars a pair of tubes with a lens at either end that you look through to see things far away (often used by bird-watchers). The lenses make things look bigger.

bird of prey a bird that hunts other animals for food

conserve to protect wildlife from being damaged or destroyed by the activities of humans

courtship an animal's behaviour that attracts a mate

extinct no longer any left alive

eyrie an eagle's nest

habitat the place where an animal lives

incubation when something is kept warm

Latin an old language spoken by the ancient Romans

poisoned killed or injured using a harmful substance

prey an animal that is hunted by other animals for food

talon the curved claw of a bird of prey, such as an eagle

territory an area where an eagle spends its life and where it finds all of its food

thermal a current of warm air that rises into the air

wingspan the distance from the tip of one of a bird's wings to the tip of the other

Index